W9-AWS-769

Substituting Ingredients

"A book [that] no experienced, as well as beginning, cook should be without. . . . The authors also provide remedies for kitchen disasters most cookbooks blithely assume will never happen."

—*Santa Barbara* (CA) *News-Press*

"At one time or another, we all have decided to make something, looked into our cupboard and discovered a missing ingredient. Now, there's help at hand. . . . *Substituting Ingredients* is the most comprehensive substitution list that I have seen."

—*New Haven* (CT) *Register*

"If you've ever started to bake and discovered when you're elbow-deep in flour that you're out of an ingredient, have I got a book for you. . . . I'm putting this book in a kitchen drawer where it will be handy when I need it."

—*Las Vegas Sun*

Substituting Ingredients

An A to Z Kitchen Reference

THIRD EDITION

by
Becky Sue Epstein
and
Hilary Dole Klein

The Globe Pequot Press

Guilford, Connecticut

Text illustrations by Kathy Michalov/Pen & Ink

Library of Congress Cataloging-in-Publication Data
Epstein, Becky Sue, 1952–
  Substituting ingredients: an A to Z kitchen reference / by Becky
Sue Epstein and Hilary Dole Klein. — 3rd ed.
    p. cm.
  Includes index.
  ISBN 1-56440-741-1
  1. Ingredient substitutions (Cookery) I. Klein, Hilary Dole, 1945–
II. Title.
TX652.E59 1996
641.5—dc20
                                                    96-3801
                                                    CIP

Manufactured in the United States of America
Third Edition/Tenth Printing

Contents

Introduction

Don't have an ingredient? *Substitute!*

Don't like something? *Substitute!*

Can't afford it? *Substitute!*

It's Sunday morning. You wake up and find yourself strangely filled with energy. You decide to make pancakes as a special treat for the family—the fluffy yet substantial kind of pancakes your mother made on Sundays. You can almost taste them. You reach for the cookbook where the recipe is marked by a turned-down, much bespattered page.

"Sour Milk Griddle Cakes," the recipe reads. You stop. Who, in his or her right mind, keeps sour milk around? You can almost feel the softness of the pancake in your mouth, smothered with real Vermont maple syrup. This is the only pancake recipe you want to use. What should you do?

It's a Friday evening. You've prepared a wonderful meal, straight out of Julia Child (well, almost), fit for a king. Fit, you hope, for an enchanting business dinner that will eventually bring you all the projects, raises, and promotions you've dreamed of. It's 7:30 P.M., and the guests are due any moment. The sauce needs only one final touch to complete its superb flavor. You reach for the cognac to dash in the required two tablespoons. Then you stop. You recall cousin Don finished off the cognac last weekend. What now?

Whether on a deserted island, in a rented vacation cottage, or at home with no time for a trip to the store, everyone has, at

some time, been in this predicament: The recipe you're making calls for an ingredient you don't happen to have on hand.

After becoming frantic with problems like this once too often, we decided to do something about it and came up with something that we, as well as our friends, could benefit by: a book of substitutions. A year of research, questioning, and testing later, the first edition appeared. For the second edition we added ingredients required for newly popular American regional and international cuisines, including Cajun, Mexican, Central American, Southeast Asian, French Provincial, Italian country, and Pacific Rim. We also incorporated ingredient equivalents into the text.

As we prepared the third edition, we continued to improve upon this handy kitchen reference. Over the past few years, the frontiers of taste have expanded enormously—and delightfully. But who among us hasn't been tempted by a recipe, only to be defeated by the challenge of coming up with a certain ingredient? We believe no cook should ever abandon an appetizing dish for lack of a particular flavoring, herb or spice. So here is an even more comprehensive compilation of substitutes. Our choices are, for the most part, very close equivalents, although in a few cases they will result in a slight alteration of flavor, by no means incompatible.

Our search began as a curiosity but turned into a passionate quest. Our tools have been common sense, ingenuity, research, testing and, of course, good taste.

With this handy reference in your kitchen, you need never despair. We have it covered, from adzuki beans and allspice to zaatar and zucchini. Just look up the next best thing and carry on with your cooking and baking.

Remember: It is better to substitute than to omit.

Tips for Successful Substituting

Here are a few general things to note for successful results when substituting.

❖ Where several substitutes are given, we've tried to list them beginning with the best-tasting and best-functioning equivalent; but use your own preferences as a guide.

❖ It's important to remember that substitutions which work in the oven may not work on top of the stove. And vice versa.

Baking

Certain substitutions are standard in baking recipes, one of the most obvious being that margarine can be used in place of shortening or butter without noticeably affecting the texture of the baked goods.

Baking times may vary, depending on the substitution, so be sure to monitor items and test for doneness.

When making substitutions in baking, try to keep the ratio of liquid ingredients to dry ingredients as close as possible to the original recipe.

Dairy Products

Except when needed for whipping, heavy cream and light cream can be used interchangeably. Yogurt or sour cream can be used for a tangier taste or a different fat content, although it's

generally not a good idea to boil yogurt or sour cream because they can separate.

Fruits

When you're making a pie, one berry can be as flavorful as the next. And limes are as good as lemons in any recipe we can think of. Both are indispensable—a splash of either juice, for instance, will keep cut fruits and vegetables from turning brown.

We have substituted fruits by taste, which seemed the most appropriate method, especially when preparing non-baked items like drinks, salads, and sorbets. For cooking and baking, you will find that a fruit's size and textural differences affect cooking times and may alter the amount of fruit to be used in the recipe. For apples, especially, the type is important, both for taste and texture.

Herbs, Spices, and Flavorings

In general, 1 tablespoon of fresh herbs equals 1 teaspoon of dried herbs. When using dried herbs, crush them in the palm of your hand to release their flavors. If using dried substitutions, cook the dish 15 minutes after adding, then taste.

Wines and spirits are often used to add flavor. The alcohol evaporates quickly during cooking. For both red and white wines, stick to the drier, rather than sweet, varieties. Madeira, sherry, and port are used to add sweetness to specific cooking and baking recipes.

Make Your Own

You will notice recipes for common condiments, sauces, spice mixtures, and more, throughout the book. Be adventurous and try them!

Substituting Ingredients
A to Z

A

Acorn Squash

= butternut squash

= pumpkin

Adzuki Beans or Chinese Red Beans

= bean paste (miso) or bean curd (tofu), used sweetened for desserts

Agar-Agar

= gelatin

Alfalfa Sprouts

= watercress

See Sprouts

Allspice

= ¼ teaspoon cinnamon plus ½ teaspoon ground cloves plus ¼ teaspoon nutmeg, in baking

= black pepper, in cooking

❖ Almonds ❖

1 lb. shelled = 1 to 1½ cups

1 lb. in shells = 3½ cups

Amaranth

See Greens

Angel Hair Pasta

See Pasta

Angostura Bitters

= cinnamon, cloves, mace, nutmeg, orange and/or
lemon peel, prunes, and rum (a secret formula)

Anise

= fennel

= dill

= cumin

Anise Seed

= fennel seed

= star anise

= caraway seed (use more)

= chervil (use a lot more)

Apples, chopped, 1 cup

= 1 cup firm pears, chopped, plus 1 tablespoon lemon juice

❖ Apples ❖

1 lb. = 2 large apples

1 lb. = $2\frac{1}{2}$ to 3 cups, sliced

Apples, sweet/mild

golden delicious

New Zealand Fuji

red delicious

Rome

russet

Apples, tart

Granny Smith

Gravenstein

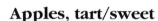

Apples, tart/sweet

Jonathan

McIntosh

New Zealand Braeburn

pippin

Winesap

Arrowroot

= cornstarch

= flour, up to a few tablespoons, for thickening

= brown rice flour

See Flour

Artichoke Hearts

= chayote, cooked and seasoned

= Jerusalem artichoke, also known as sunchoke

= kohlrabi, cooked

Arugula or Rocket

= Belgian endive

= endive

= escarole

= dandelion greens

Asafetida

= equal parts onion powder, celery seed, curry powder and cumin

Asian Pears

= pears

Azafran or Safflower

= saffron (use only a tiny bit)

B

Bacon

= smoked ham, in cooking

Baking Powder, 1 teaspoon double-acting

= ½ teaspoon cream of tartar plus ¼ teaspoon baking soda

= ¼ teaspoon baking soda plus ½ cup sour milk or cream or buttermilk; reduce some other liquid from recipe

= ¼ teaspoon baking soda plus 2 more eggs if recipe calls for sweet milk; reduce some other liquid from recipe

= 4 teaspoons quick-cooking tapioca

❖ Bananas ❖

1 lb. = 3 to 4 whole

1 lb. = 2 cups, mashed

Barbecue Sauce

½ cup vinegar

1 cup ketchup

½ cup onion, chopped

½ teaspoon cayenne pepper

½ cup brown sugar

2 teaspoons dry mustard

2 tablespoons Worcestershire sauce

½ cup vegetable oil

½ teaspoon salt (optional)

2 tablespoons liquid smoke (optional)

Combine ingredients. Simmer for 30 minutes, if desired. Yields 2⅓ cups.

Basil, dried

= tarragon

= summer savory

Basmati Rice

= long-grain white rice

Bay Leaf

= thyme

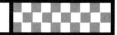

Beach Plum

= crab apple

= quince

❖ Beans, dried ❖

1 lb. = 1½ to 2 cups

1 lb = 5 to 6 cups cooked

1 cup = 2 to 2½ cups canned

Bean Sprouts

= celery

See Sprouts

Beef, ground

= ground turkey

= ground pork

= ground veal

= ground lamb

Note: Combinations of beef and these substitutes can also be used in most recipes.

Beet Greens

See Greens

Belgian Endive
= fennel

See Lettuce

Bermuda Onions
See Onions (Sweet)

Blackberries
= boysenberries

= loganberries

= raspberries

Black Pepper
= white pepper

= allspice in cooking, especially if salt is used in dish

Black Peppercorns
= white peppercorns

Note: Peppercorns vary in strength.

Blueberries
= huckleberries

= elderberries

Bok Choy or Pakchoi or Chinese Cabbage
= Napa cabbage

= savoy cabbage

= green cabbage

Boniato or Batata or White Sweet Potatoes

= sweet potatoes

= plantains

Borage

= cucumber, especially in dishes with yogurt

Bouquet Garni

= 3 sprigs parsley, 1 sprig thyme, 1 bay leaf.

Optional: 1 sprig each of basil, celery leaf, fennel, marjoram, or tarragon. Tie up with string or cheesecloth.

Bourbon

= whiskey

Boysenberries

= blackberries

= raspberries

Brandy

= cognac

= whiskey

❖ Bread ❖

1 lb. = 10 to 14 slices

1 slice = ½ cup soft bread crumbs

1 slice = ¼ to ⅓ cup dry bread crumbs

Bread Crumbs, dry, ¼ cup

- = ¼ cup cracker crumbs
- = ½ slice bread, cubed, toasted, and crumbled
- = ¼ cup rolled oats
- = ⅓ cup soft bread crumbs
- = ¼ cup matzoh meal
- = ¼ cup flour
- = ¼ cup crushed corn flakes

Breadfruit

- = potatoes

Broccoli Rabe or Italian Turnip

See Greens

Broth, Beef, 1 cup

- = 1 bouillon cube plus 1 cup water
- = 1 cup beef stock
- = 1 cup beef consommé

Broth, Chicken, 1 cup

- = 1 bouillon cube plus 1 cup water
- = 1 cup chicken stock

Bulgur

- = cracked wheat
- = buckwheat or kasha
- = brown rice
- = couscous
- = millet
- = quinoa

Burdock (Root) or Gobo

- = parsnip

Butter, for frying

- = oil
- = bacon grease (this will flavor food, too)

Butter, in baking

- = margarine
- = shortening
- = applesauce
- = prune purée

Note: Oil is generally not interchangeable with butter in baking.

Butter, 1 cup

- = 1 cup margarine
- = ⅞ cup vegetable shortening
- = ⅞ cup lard
- = ⅞ cup cottonseed oil
- = ⅞ cup nut oil
- = ⅞ cup corn oil
- = ⅔ cup chicken fat (not for baking or sweets)
- = ⅞ cup solid shortening

Note: For softened butter, or to stretch butter, blend ½ cup corn oil or safflower oil into 1 lb. butter; refrigerate.

❖ Butter ❖

1 lb. = 4 sticks

1 lb. = 2 cups

1 cup = 2 sticks

1 stick = ½ cup

2 tablespoons = ¼ stick

2 tablespoons = 1 ounce

4 tablespoons = ½ stick

4 tablespoons = 2 ounces

8 tablespoons = 1 stick

8 tablespoons = 4 ounces

16 tablespoons = 2 sticks

16 tablespoons = 8 ounces

Buttermilk

- = 1 cup milk plus 1¾ tablespoons cream of tartar
- = sour cream
- = plain, low-fat yogurt

Butternut Squash

- = acorn squash
- = pumpkin
- = buttercup squash

C

Cabbage

See Chinese Cabbage, Green Cabbage, Red Cabbage, Savoy Cabbage

---

❖ Cabbage ❖

1 lb. = 4 cups shredded raw

1 lb. = 2 cups cooked

Cactus or Nopal

- = green pepper
- = okra

Cactus Pears

= kiwi

= watermelon

Cajun Seasoning

2 teaspoons cayenne (or paprika for a milder version)

2 teaspoons thyme

2 teaspoons oregano

1 teaspoon cumin

1 teaspoon mustard powder

1 teaspoon ground black pepper

2 cloves garlic

1 onion

2 teaspoons salt

Mix in a food processor or with a mortar and pestle.

Calabazo or West Indian Pumpkin or Cuban Squash

= winter squash

= pumpkin

Callaloo

= spinach

= chard

= turnip greens

See Greens

Capers

= chopped green olives

= pickled, green nasturtium seeds

Capon

= large roasting chicken

Caraway Seed

= fennel seed

= cumin seed

Cardamom

= cinnamon

= mace

Cardoon or Cardoni

= artichoke heart

Carrots

= parsnips

❖ Carrots ❖

1 lb. = 3 cups shredded or sliced raw

Cassava

= potato

Cassia

= cinnamon

Cauliflower

= kohlrabi

Cayenne Pepper

= hot red pepper, ground

= chili powder

Celeriac or Celery Root

= parsnip (cooked)

= jicama (raw)

= celery

Celery

= green pepper

= jicama

= bean sprouts

= Belgian endive

= fennel

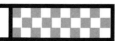

❖ Celery ❖

1 stalk = ⅓ cup diced

Celery Root

See Celeriac

Celery Seed

= dill seed

Cèpe (Porcini or Boletus) Mushrooms

= shiitake mushrooms

See Mushrooms

Chanterelle Mushrooms

= pied de mouton or hedgehog mushrooms

See Mushrooms

Chard

See Greens

Chayote Squash or Mirliton or Christophine Squash

= yellow squash

= large zucchini, cooked

= green peppers, when cooked and stuffed

= fuzzy melon

❖ Cheese ❖

4 oz. = 1 cup shredded

Cheese

Within each group, these cheeses can be substituted for each other.

fontina

Havarti

Monterey Jack

muenster

Port-Salut

American

cheddar

colby

longhorn

Edam

Gouda

bleu (blue) cheese

Roquefort

Emmenthaler
Gruyère
Jarlsberg
raclette
Swiss

mozzarella (for cooking not buffalo mozzarella)
provolone

Brie
Camenbert

Gorgonzola
Stilton

Parmesan
pecorino
Romano

buffalo milk mozzarella
mozzarella (not for cooking)

chèvre or goat (white)
feta

Cheese, *continued*

    cottage cheese

    cream cheese

    farmer cheese

    hoop cheese

    mascarpone

    ricotta

    yogurt (especially in dips)

Cheese Topping for Popcorn

¼ cup Parmesan cheese

¼ cup grated blue cheese

1 teaspoon paprika

½ teaspoon garlic powder

½ teaspoon onion powder or onion salt

Sprinkle on popped popcorn. Warm briefly in microwave or oven before serving.

Cherimoya

    = custard apples

    = soursop (or sweetsop)

    = pears, pineapples and bananas with lemon or lime juice

    = melons and peaches

    = guavas and peaches

Chervil

- = parsley
- = tarragon (use less)
- = anise (use less)
- = Italian parsley

See Lettuce

Chicken, pieces

- = turkey
- = Cornish game hen
- = rabbit

Chicken Breasts, boneless

- = turkey breast slices
- = veal scallops

Chicory

See Lettuce

Chile (or Chili) Oil or Red Pepper Oil

3 tablespoons sesame oil

3 to 4 spicy red peppers

Heat oil. Fry peppers until they turn dark. Remove peppers and discard. Use the remaining oil.

Chile or Chili Peppers, hot

- = habanero
- = Fresno
- = jalapeño
- = serrano

Chile or Chili Peppers, milder

- = Anaheim or chile verde
- = banana peppers or Hungarian wax peppers
- = pepperoncini
- = poblano (called ancho when dried)

Note: Chili peppers vary greatly in strength from mild to extra-hot, so use care when attempting substitutions.

Chili Paste

See Indonesian Sambal

Chili Powder

- = cayenne pepper (*Optional:* add cumin, oregano, garlic, and other spices)

Chinese Cabbage

- = cabbage
- = lettuce

Chinese Parsley

See Cilantro

Chives

- = green onion tops
- = onion powder (use small amount)
- = leeks
- = shallots (use less)

❖ Baking Chocolate ❖

1 square = 1 oz.

Chocolate, Baking, unsweetened, 1 ounce or square

- = 3 tablespoons unsweetened cocoa plus 1 tablespoon butter or margarine
- = 3 tablespoons carob powder plus 2 tablespoons water

Chocolate, Baking, unsweetened pre-melted, 1 ounce

- = 3 tablespoons unsweetened cocoa plus 1 tablespoon oil or melted shortening

Chocolate, Semi-sweet, 6 ounces chips, bits, or squares

- = 9 tablespoons cocoa plus 7 tablespoons sugar plus 3 tablespoons butter or margarine

Chocolate, White

Note: There is no exact substitute for white chocolate.

Chocolate, White, chips

= semi-sweet or milk chocolate chips, in cookies or cakes

❖ Chocolate Chips ❖

1 12-oz. package = 2 cups

Chutney

1 8-ounce jar apricot or peach preserves

1 clove garlic, minced, or ½ teaspoon garlic powder

½ teaspoon powdered ginger, or 1 tablespoon fresh or candied ginger, minced

½ teaspoon salt

1 tablespoon apple cider vinegar

½ cup raisins (optional)

Combine ingredients. Yields 1½ cups.

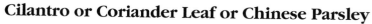
Cilantro or Coriander Leaf or Chinese Parsley

- = parsley and lemon juice
- = orange peel with a little sage
- = lemon grass with a little mint
- = parsley with mint
- = Italian parsley (for looks)

Cinnamon

- = allspice (use less)
- = cardamom

Clementines

- = tangerines
- = mandarin oranges

Cloves, ground

- = allspice
- = nutmeg
- = mace

Club Soda

- = mineral water
- = seltzer

Cockles

- = small clams

Cocktail Sauce

2 tablespoons horseradish

½ cup ketchup

1½ teaspoons Worcestershire sauce (optional)

2 tablespoons lemon juice (optional)

black pepper (optional)

bottled hot sauce (to taste; optional)

½ cup chili sauce (optional)

Combine ingredients.

Coconut, grated

Note: If less than ½ cup, can be omitted from recipe.

Coconut Milk, fresh, thick, 1 cup

= 4 to 5 tablespoons coconut cream, solidified, dissolved in 1 cup hot water or milk

= 1 cup top layer of canned cream of coconut liquid

= 1 cup medium cream with 1 teaspoon coconut flavoring

Coconut Milk, fresh, thin, 1 cup

- = 2 tablespoons coconut cream, solidified, dissolved in 1 cup hot water or milk
- = 1 cup canned cream of coconut liquid
- = 1 cup whole milk with 1 teaspoon coconut flavoring
- = 1 cup milk beaten with 3 tablespoons grated coconut

❖ Coffee ❖

½ cup strong brewed = 1 teaspoon instant in ½ cup water

1 lb. ground = 80 tablespoons

1 lb. ground = 30 to 40 cups (servings)

Cognac

- = brandy
- = whiskey

Collard Greens

See Greens

Condensed Milk, Sweetened

1 cup instant powdered milk

⅓ cup hot water

½ cup sugar

1 tablespoon melted butter or margarine

Mix ingredients in blender until smooth. Refrigerate.

Coriander Leaf

See Cilantro

Coriander Seed, ground

= caraway plus cumin

= lemon plus sage

= allspice with a pinch of lemon or lemon zest

❖ Corn ❖

6 ears = 2 to 3 cups kernels

Corn Flour

= flour, up to a few tablespoons, for thickening

See Flour

Cornish Game Hen

= squab

= quail

= chicken

Cornmeal

= (corn) grits

= polenta

Cornstarch

= flour, up to a few tablespoons, for thickening

See Flour

Corn Syrup, light, 1 cup

= 1¼ cups sugar plus ⅓ cup liquid, boiled together till syrupy

Cos

See Lettuce (Romaine)

❖ Cottage Cheese ❖

1 lb. = 2 cups

Cottage Cheese

See Cheese (Cottage)

Couscous

= bulgur (cracked wheat)

= quinoa

= kasha

= millet

= orzo

= rice

Crayfish

= small lobster

= prawns

= langouste (langoustine)

Cream, Clotted

= heavy cream, whipped to soft peaks

= sour cream with a pinch of baking soda

= crème fraiche

Cream, Heavy, not for whipping, 1 cup

= ¾ cup milk plus ¼ cup shortening or butter

= ⅔ cup evaporated milk

❖ Heavy or Whipping Cream ❖

1 cup = 2 cups whipped

Cream, Light (or Half and Half), 1 cup

= ½ cup heavy cream plus ½ cup milk

= ⅞ cup milk plus 3 tablespoons butter or margarine

= ½ cup evaporated milk plus ½ cup milk

Cream, Whipped, sweetened, 1 cup

= 1 4-ounce package frozen whipped cream topping

= 1 envelope whipped topping mix, prepared as directed

= 1 mashed banana beaten with 1 stiffly beaten egg white plus 1 teaspoon sugar

= 1 cup nonfat dry milk powder whipped with 1 cup ice water and sweetened to taste (this is for low-calorie desserts and drinks; it will not hold firm)

= ice-cold evaporated milk, plus 2 teaspoons sugar, whipped (use immediately)

Cream Cheese

= cottage cheese blended with cream or cream with a little butter and/or milk to correct consistency

Crème Fraiche

- = sour cream, in recipes
- = ½ sour cream and ½ heavy cream

Crème Fraiche

1 cup heavy cream
½ cup buttermilk or sour cream
or sour milk or yogurt

Stir well in glass container. To make firm crème fraiche, let sit in a warm place for 6 hours and then refrigerate. Yields 1½ cups.

Cumin

- = caraway plus anise
- = fennel

Currants

- = gooseberries

Currants, 1 cup (dried)

- = 1 cup raisins
- = 1 cup soft prunes or dates, finely chopped

Note: If less than ½ cup, can be omitted from recipe.

Curry Powder

2 tablespoons ground coriander

2 tablespoons cumin

2 tablespoons red pepper

2 tablespoons turmeric

2 tablespoons ground ginger

Optional: allspice, black pepper, cinnamon, ground fennel, fenugreek, garlic powder, mace, mustard powder

Combine. Yields ⅔ cup.

Custard Apples

= cherimoya

= soursop (or sweetsop)

= melons and peaches

= guavas and peaches

D

Daikon

= jicama

= radish

Dandelion Greens

See Greens, Lettuce

Dasheen

= sweet potato or yam

❖ Dates ❖

1 lb. = 2⅔ cups chopped, pitted

Dates

= raisins

= figs

= prunes

Note: If less than ½ cup, can be omitted from recipe.

Delicata Squash

= butternut squash plus sweet potato

Dill Seed

= caraway

= celery seed

E

Edible Blossoms, for garnish and in salads

bachelor buttons

blue borage

calendula petals

chive blossoms

Johnny-jump-ups

marigolds

mini carnations

nasturtiums

pansies

rocket

rose petals

snap dragons

sweet pea

violets

wild radish

❖ Eggs ❖

1 cup = 4 to 5 large

1 cup = 8 to 10 whites

1 cup = 10 to 12 yolks

Eggs, for scrambling

= tofu, lightly chopped

Eggs, Whole

= 2 tablespoons liquid plus 2 tablespoons flour plus ½ tablespoon shortening plus ½ teaspoon baking powder

= 2 yolks plus 1 tablespoon water

= 2 yolks, in custards, sauces, or similar mixtures

= 2 tablespoons oil plus 1 tablespoon water

= 1 teaspoon cornstarch plus 3 tablespoons more liquid in recipe

Note: If halving recipe, do not try to halve one egg; use one whole egg. If short one *more* egg in recipe, substitute 1 teaspoon vinegar or 1 teaspoon baking powder.

Elderberries

= blueberries

= huckleberries

Elephant Garlic

= garlic (use less)

Endive or Curly Endive

= Belgian endive

= chicory

= escarole

See Lettuce

Enoki (Enokitake) Mushrooms

= oyster mushrooms

See Mushrooms

Escarole

= arugula

= endive

= chicory

Evaporated Milk

= light cream or half and half

= heavy cream

F

Fava Beans

= lima beans, especially baby lima beans

Feijoa

See Pineapple Guava

Fennel, bulb or Florentine

= Belgian endive

= celery

Fennel Seed

= anise seed or star anise

= caraway seed

Fiddlehead Fern

See Greens

❖ Figs ❖

1 lb. = 2⅔ cups chopped

Note: If less than ½ cup, can be omitted from recipe.

Filé Powder

See Gumbo Filé

Fines Herbes

Equal amounts of parsley, tarragon, chervil, and chives, minced together.

Fish Fillets

bass or sea bass, also known as Mexican bass or Chilean bass

bluefish

carp

catfish

cod

coho salmon, also known as salmon trout

flounder

grouper

haddock

halibut

ling cod

John Dory

mahimahi

monkfish, also known as lotte

muskellunge, also known as muskie

nilefish

orange roughy

pickerel

pike

plaice

pollock

red snapper

rock cod

rockfish

Fish Fillets, continued

salmon

sandab

scrod (this is a type of catch, not a type of fish)

shark (dogfish)

sole

striped bass

talapia or St. Peter's fish

trout

turbot

walleyed pike

whitefish

Fish Steaks

ahi

albacore

cod

halibut

John Dory

mackerel

ono

salmon

sea bass

shark

swordfish

tuna

Fish, Whole

bass

catfish

flounder

halibut

mackerel

muskellunge

perch

pike

salmon

smelt

trout

turbot

Fish Sauce (Asian)

= 1 part soy sauce blended with 4 parts mashed anchovies

Five-Spice Powder, for Asian Cooking

1 teaspoon ground star anise

1 teaspoon ground fennel seed

1 teaspoon ground Szechwan pepper

½ teaspoon ground cassia or cinnamon

½ teaspoon ground cloves

Flavorings (extracts and aromatics)

Commonly available; some are imitation:

almond

anise

banana

brandy

butter

cherry

chocolate

coconut

lemon

liquid smoke

maple

orange

peppermint

pineapple

root beer

rose water

rum

vanilla

See Liqueurs

❖ Flour ❖

1 lb. white = 3½ to 4 cups

1 cup white = 1 cup plus 2 tablespoons cake flour

1 lb. cake = 4 to 4½ cups

1 cup cake = ⅞ cup white flour

1 lb. whole wheat = 3 cups sifted

Flour, for thickening, up to a few tablespoons only

= Bisquick

= tapioca, quick cooking

= cornstarch or corn flour (use less)

= arrowroot (use less)

= brown rice flour or soy flour or rye flour

= potato starch or potato flour

= mashed potatoes, flakes or prepared

= 1 whole egg or 2 yolks or 2 whites (especially for cooked sauces)—whisk continuously

= pancake mix, for frying pork chops or chicken

Flour, Graham

= whole wheat flour

Flour, Self-rising, 1 cup

= 1 cup flour plus ¼ teaspoon baking powder

Optional: add a pinch of salt

Flour, White, for baking, 1 cup

= 1 cup plus 2 tablespoons cake flour

= ¾ cup whole wheat flour; reduce shortening to ⅔ the amount for cookies; add 1 or 2 more tablespoons liquid for cakes; add more for bread.

Note: Whole wheat flour will make the product denser (heavier); it's advisable to start out substituting half whole wheat or other grain flours. Rye, for instance, has a nutty flavor. Soy can also be used for extra protein; substitute ¹⁄₁₀ to ¼ soy flour for wheat flour.

Flour, Whole Wheat, 1 cup

= 1 cup graham flour

= 2 tablespoons wheat germ plus enough white flour to make 1 cup.

Note: Product may be less dense or lighter when using white flour.

Flowers

See Edible Blossoms

Focaccio Bread

= baked pizza dough

Fuzzy Melon or Hairy Cucumber

= zucchini

G

Galangal or Laos Powder

= ginger root or powdered ginger plus cardamom

Garam Masala, for Indian cooking

2 teaspoons ground cardamom

5 teaspoons ground coriander

4 teaspoons ground cumin

1 teaspoon ground cloves

2 teaspoons black pepper

1 teaspoon ground cinnamon

1 teaspoon ground nutmeg

Combine. Yields ⅓ cup

Garlic, 1 clove

= ½ teaspoon minced, dried garlic

= ¼ teaspoon garlic powder

= ¼ teaspoon garlic juice

= ½ teaspoon garlic salt (and omit ½ teaspoon salt from recipe)

= garlic chives (use more)

= elephant garlic (use more)

❖ Garlic ❖

1 clove garlic = ½ to 1 teaspoon chopped garlic

Garlic Butter

1 clove garlic, mashed

4 tablespoons salted butter, creamed or melted

Combine. Yields ¼ cup.

Garlic, Green

= leeks

Ghee

= clarified butter

Ginger, fresh, grated

= powdered ginger (use less) plus a little white pepper and lemon juice

= minced, crystalized ginger with sugar washed off

Ginger, powdered

= mace plus lemon peel

Gooseberries

= currants

Green Beans

= haricots verts

= wax beans

Green Cabbage

= Savoy cabbage

= Chinese cabbage

= kohlrabi

= lettuce

= brussel sprouts, shredded (in stir fries)

Green Onions

= scallions

= leeks

= shallots (use less)

= chives

Green Peppercorns

= white or black peppercorns (use less and do not leave in food)

= cracked pepper (use less)

❖ Green Peppers ❖

1 large = 1 cup diced

Green Peppers

= yellow peppers

= red peppers

= celery

Greens, mild in flavor

amaranth

beet greens

bok choy

collard greens

Greens, medium in flavor

callaloo

kale

spinach

Swiss chard, also known as chard

turnip greens

Greens, strong in flavor

    broccoli rabe, also known as rapini

    dandelion greens

    fiddlehead fern

    mustard greens

    nettles

    sorrel

    turnip greens

Grits (corn)

    = cornmeal

    = polenta

Guavas

    = pears with nutmeg and lime juice

    = strawberry plus pineapple plus banana

Gumbo Filé

    = sassafras

H

Haricots Verts

    = young green beans

Harissa Sauce (Tunisian Hot Sauce)

1 whole head of garlic, peeled

6 small red chilies (if dried, soak first)

1 tablespoon ground coriander

1 tablespoon ground cumin

1 tablespoon caraway seeds

1 tablespoon dried mint

1 tablespoon olive oil

1 teaspoon salt

3 tablespoons (or more) fresh coriander

Blend in a food processor.

Herb Butter

½ teaspoon parsley

½ teaspoon chives

½ teaspoon tarragon

½ teaspoon shallots

4 tablespoons salted butter, creamed

Combine. Yields ⅓ cup.

Herbes de Provence

1 teaspoon fresh thyme

1 teaspoon fresh summer savory

½ teaspoon fresh lavender

¼ teaspoon fresh rosemary

Optional: ¼ teaspoon fresh fennel, ¼ teaspoon fresh basil, ½ teaspoon fresh oregano, and/or ¼ teaspoon fresh sage

Mince together. Once prepared, herbs may be used fresh or dried.

❖ Honey ❖

1 lb. = 1⅓ cups

Honey, in baking, 1 cup

= 1¼ cups sugar plus ¼ cup more liquid

Note: This may cause the product to brown faster and may necessitate a lower oven temperature.

Honey Butter

1 tablespoon honey

3 tablespoons unsalted butter, creamed

Combine. Yields ¼ cup.

Honey Mustard

2 tablespoons honey

3 tablespoons prepared yellow mustard

Combine. Yields ¼ cup.

Horseradish, fresh, grated

= daikon radish

= wasabi

Hot Fudge Sauce

1 egg, slightly beaten

1 cup sugar

¼ cup cream

2 squares unsweetened baking chocolate

1 tablespoon butter

1 teaspoon vanilla

Melt first 4 ingredients slowly over low heat. Bring to a boil. Cool a minute. Beat in butter and vanilla. Serve warm over ice cream. Yields 1½ cups.

Bittersweet Hot Fudge Sauce

4 squares unsweetened baking chocolate

3 tablespoons butter

⅔ cup water

1¾ cups sugar

¾ cup corn syrup

1 teaspoon vanilla or rum

Melt butter and chocolate slowly over low heat. Add water, sugar, and corn syrup. Boil 10 minutes. Allow to cool a bit. Beat in the vanilla or rum. Serve warm. Yields 2½ cups.

Hot Pepper Jelly

1 cup apple jelly

1½ small, hot chilies or 2 tablespoons canned chili peppers

Combine. Process in a food processor. Yields 1 cup.

Hot Pepper Sauce

- = bottled hot sauce
- = Tabasco sauce
- = ground red pepper
- = cayenne pepper
- = hot red pepper flakes
- = chili powder

Hot Red Pepper Flakes

- = chopped, dried red pepper pods
- = red pepper (use less)

Huckleberries

- = blueberries
- = elderberries

I

Indonesian Sambal (Chili Paste)

2 cloves garlic

½ cup dried hot red chilies, seeded

1 onion sliced

4 tablespoons sugar

4 tablespoons lemon juice

4 tablespoons water

Blend ingredients in a food processor and then simmer for 10 minutes. Let cool before serving.

Italian Seasoning

1 tablespoon oregano, dried or fresh

1 tablespoon thyme, dried or fresh

1 tablespoon sage, dried or fresh

1 tablespoon parsley, dried or fresh

1 tablespoon black pepper, ground

2 bay leaves, crushed into small pieces

J

Jackfruit

See Breadfruit

Jaggery, 1 cup

= ½ cup white sugar plus ½ cup brown sugar

Japanese Pears

See Asian Pears

Jerusalem Artichokes or Sunchokes

= artichoke hearts

Jicama

= daikon

= raw turnip

= water chestnut

Juniper Berries

= a small amount of gin, boiled for a few minutes

= bay leaves plus caraway seeds plus chopped mint

K

Kabocha Squash

= buttercup squash

= butternut squash

= acorn squash

Kale

See Greens

Ketchup

½ cup tomato sauce

2 tablespoons sugar

2 tablespoons vinegar

½ teaspoon salt

⅛ teaspoon ground cloves

or

½ cup tomato sauce

½ cup tomato paste

¼ cup sugar

3 tablespoons vinegar

1 teaspoon salt

Combine. Yields 1 cup.

Kidney Beans

= pink beans

= pinto beans

= red beans

Note: These substitutes are smaller beans.

Kiwi Fruit

= strawberries with a little lime juice

Note: Use only fresh berries.

Kohlrabi

= cauliflower

= artichoke heart

= broccoli stems

= cabbage

= celeriac

= radish

= turnip

Kudzu

= beets

Kumquat

= orange plus lime plus bergamot

L

Leeks

- = shallots
- = green onions
- = onions (use less)

❖ Lemon ❖

1 medium = 2 to 3 tablespoons juice
1 medium = 1 tablespoon grated rind (zest)

Lemons

- = limes

Lemon, as flavoring

- = lime
- = lemongrass
- = verbena

Lemongrass

- = lemon zest
- = verbena
- = lemon juice

Lemon Juice

- = vinegar
- = lime juice
- = crushed Vitamin C pills mixed with water to taste (for small amounts)

Lemon Peel, grated

- = equal amount of marmalade
- = equal amount of lime or orange peel

Note: If less than 1 tablespoon, can be omitted from recipe, especially if another flavoring or essence is used.

See Flavorings

Lentils

- = yellow split peas

Lettuce and Salad Greens, buttery and soft

bibb, also known as limestone

Boston, also known as butterhead

green leaf

mâche, also known as lamb's lettuce or corn salad

oak leaf

red leaf

Lettuce and Salad Greens, crisp and crunchy

iceberg, also known as crisphead

purslane

romaine, also known as cos

salad bowl

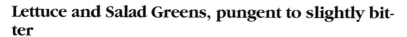

Lettuce and Salad Greens, pungent to slightly bitter

arugula, also known as rocket

Belgian endive

chervil

chicory, also known as curly endive or frisée

dandelion greens

escarole

mizuna

mustard greens

nasturtium leaves

pepper grass, also known as garden cress

radicchio

sorrel

watercress

Lima Beans

= fava beans

Limes

= lemons

Lime Juice

= lemon juice

Lingonberries

= cranberries

= red currants

Liqueurs

Standard liqueur flavors include:

Mint – Creme de Menthe

Orange – Curaçao, Grand Marnier, Cointreau

Raspberry – Cassis, Chambord

Anise (or licorice) – Pastis, Ouzo, Pernod, Arak

Note: One liqueur can be used in place of two in a recipe.

Loganberries

= blackberries

= boysenberries

= raspberries

Lovage

= celery leaves plus curry powder or ground pepper

= chervil

= coriander

See Greens, Lettuce

Lychee

= peeled grapes

M

❖ Macaroni ❖

1 lb. elbow = 8 to 9 cups cooked

Macaroni

See Pasta

Mace

= allspice

= cloves

= nutmeg

Optional: add cardamom

Mâche

= arugula

= spinach

See Lettuce

Madeira

- = sherry
- = port
- = Marsala
- = sweet vermouth

Mango

- = peach with a little lemon and allspice

❖ Margarine ❖

1 lb. = 4 sticks

1 lb. = 2 cups

1 stick = ½ cup

Margarine

- = butter
- = shortening

See Butter

Marinade for Beef, Lamb, or Chicken

1 cup red wine or red wine vinegar for beef or lamb; or 1 cup dry white wine for chicken

1 cup salad oil or olive oil or combination

2 cloves garlic

1 teaspoon black pepper, freshly ground

¼ cup minced fresh parsley

½ teaspoon dried thyme

½ teaspoon dried marjoram

1 bay leaf

Optional: 1 small onion; chopped, 1 small carrot, chopped; 2 allspice berries, whole; 1 teaspoon salt; ½ teaspoon dried rosemary

Combine ingredients. Yields 2½ to 3 cups.

Marinade for Fish or Chicken

1½ cups soy sauce

1¾ cups ketchup (optional)

¼ cup dry red wine

2 tablespoons fresh grated ginger

2 tablespoons brown sugar

1 small onion, finely chopped

juice of 1 lemon (2 to 3 tablespoons)

dash of bottled hot sauce

2 cloves garlic, mashed

Combine ingredients. Yields 4¼ cups.

Marinade for Pork

1½ cups dry white wine

3 tablespoons olive oil

1 small onion, chopped

1 bay leaf

2 whole cloves

½ teaspoon dried thyme

Optional: 1 small carrot, chopped; 2 allspice berries, whole; 2 juniper berries, whole

Combine ingredients. Yields 2 to 2½ cups.

Marjoram
- = oregano (use less)
- = thyme

Marsala
- = sweet vermouth
- = Madeira
- = medium sweet sherry
- = port

❖ Marshmallows ❖

1 large = 6 miniature

11 large = 1 cup

Masa Harina

= corn flour

Mascarpone

= cream cheese, whipped with a little butter and/or heavy cream

See Cheese (Mascarpone)

Matsuke Mushrooms

= morel mushrooms

See Mushrooms

Maui Onions

See Onions (Sweet)

Mayonnaise

= yogurt or sour cream, especially in small amounts and in dips

Optional: add lemon juice

Melon

= papaya

= mango

Melon, Crenshaw

= Spanish melon

Melon, Honeydew

= Casaba melon

Mexican Mint Marigold

= tarragon

Milk, Condensed

See Condensed Milk (Sweetened)

Milk, Evaporated

= light cream or half and half

= heavy cream

Milk, in baking

= fruit juice plus ½ teaspoon baking soda added to the flour

Milk, 1 cup

= 1 cup light cream (*Optional:* delete up to 4 tablespoons shortening from recipe)

= ½ cup evaporated milk plus ½ cup water

= 1 cup skim milk (*Optional:* add 2 tablespoons shortening)

= 3 tablespoons powdered milk plus 1 cup water (add 2 tablespoons butter if whole milk is required)

= soy or nut milks, in recipes

Millet

- = orzo (or other tiny pasta)
- = barley
- = quinoa

Mineral water

- = club soda
- = seltzer

Mineola

- = grapefruit plus tangerine

Mint

- = mint or spearmint tea from tea bags or bulk tea
- = crème de menthe, in sweets

Mirin (Japanese sweet rice wine)

- = sweet sherry
- = sweet vermouth

Mirliton

See Chayote

Mizuna

- = chicory or arugula

See Lettuce

Molasses, in baking, 1 cup

= ¾ cup white or brown sugar plus ¼ cup liquid,
and increase spices

Morel Mushrooms

= matsuke mushrooms

Mulled Cider Spice Blend

1 cinnamon stick broken in pieces

1 whole nutmeg cut into quarters

6 whole cloves

2 teaspoons dried lemon zest

Tie up in a piece of cheesecloth. Add to 6 cups cider and heat.

Mung Beans

= split peas

Mushrooms

See Cèpe, Chanterelle, Matsuke, Morel, Oyster, Pied de Mouton, Porcini, Shiitake

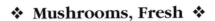
❖ Mushrooms, Fresh ❖

1 lb. = 5 cups sliced

1 lb. = 12 oz. canned, drained

1 lb. = 3 oz. dried

Mustard, Dry, 1 teaspoon

= 1 tablespoon prepared mustard from jar

Mustard Greens

See Greens, Lettuce

Mustard, Hot Chinese

= Coleman's English dry mustard, prepared with water

Prepared Mustard

1 teaspoon dry mustard

½ teaspoon water

2 drops vinegar

Mix well. Yields ½ tablespoon.

N

Nectarines

= peaches

Nigella

= poppy seeds plus black pepper

❖ Noodles ❖

1 lb. dried = 6 to 8 cups cooked

Noodles

See Pasta

Nopal

See Cactus

Nutmeg

= allspice

= cloves

= mace

❖ Nuts ❖

1 lb. shelled = 4 cups nutmeats

1 lb. in shell = 1⅔ cups nutmeats

Nuts, in baking

= bran

= soy nuts, toasted and chopped

Note: If less than ½ cup, can be omitted from recipe.

O

❖ Oats ❖

1 cup, quick cooking = 1¾ cups cooked

Oil, for cooking, interchangeable:

= canola oil

= corn oil

= light sesame oil

= olive oil

Oil, for cooking, continued

- = peanut oil (adds some flavor)
- = rice bran oil
- = safflower oil
- = soy oil
- = vegetable oil

Note: The burning temperatures of different oils, butter, and margarine vary.

Oil, for salads, flavored

- = almond oil
- = Asian sesame or dark sesame oil (mix with unflavored oil)
- = hazelnut oil
- = olive oil (use virgin)
- = walnut oil

Oil, for salads, unflavored, interchangeable

- = avocado oil
- = canola oil
- = rice bran oil
- = safflower oil
- = soy oil

Oil, for sautéing (not for deep-fat frying)

- = margarine or butter

Oil, in baking, 1 tablespoon

= 1¼ tablespoons butter

= 1¼ tablespoons margarine

= 1 tablespoon mayonnaise, in cake recipes

Note: Use these substitutions only for small amounts, up to a few tablespoons. If substituting olive or other strong oils in baking, add a few drops of mint to mask the pungency; the baked goods will have a mint flavor.

Okra

= eggplant (although texture will be different)

❖ Onion ❖

1 medium = ¾ cup chopped

Onion, White or Yellow, 1 medium or ¼ cup

= red onion, not usually used for cooking

= 1 tablespoon instant minced onion

= ¼ cup frozen chopped onion

= 1 tablespoon onion powder

= shallots (use more)

= leeks

= green onions (use more)

Onion Powder

See Onion (White or Yellow)

Onions, Sweet

Vidalia

Walla Walla

Maui

red, also called Italian red or purple

Bermuda

Spanish yellow

Orange Peel and Orange Peel, grated

= tangerine peel

= marmalade

= Grand Marnier

= Curaçao

= Cointreau

= lemon or lime peel

Note: If less than 1 tablespoon, can be omitted from recipe.

❖ Oranges ❖

1 medium = ⅓ to ½ cup juice

1 medium = 1 to 2 tablespoons peel, grated

Oregano

= marjoram

= rosemary

= thyme, fresh

Oyster Mushrooms

= button or market mushrooms

P

Pancake Syrup

= fruit jelly, melted (add water to thin)

Pancetta

= lean bacon, cooked

= prosciutto

= thinly sliced ham

Paprika

= turmeric with red or cayenne pepper

Parsley

= chervil

= tarragon

Parsley Root

= parsnip

Parsnips

= parsley root

= carrots

Passion Fruit

= pomegranates with apricot and grapefruit

= pomegranates

= lemon plus honey plus jasmine

Pasta, filled

agnolotti

ravioli

tortellini

cannelloni

manicotti

Pasta, flat

noodles

fettuccine

linguine

tagliatelle

Pasta, medium

rice noodles

spaghetti

soba (buckwheat) noodles

Oriental (ramen) noodles

Pasta, miscellaneous shapes

farfalle ("butterflies")

mostaccioli ("little mustaches")

rotelle ("wheels")

rotini ("corkscrews")

ruote ("wagon wheels")

gnocchi (miniature potato dumplings)

Pasta, thin

angel hair

bucatini

fedelini

vermicelli

fusilli

spaghettini

cappellini

Pasta, tiny

orzo

pastini

Pasta, tube

bocconcini

cannolicchi

ditali

macaroni

penne

rigatoni

ziti

❖ Pasta ❖

1 8-oz. package = 5½ cups cooked

Pattypan Squash or Summer Squash
- = yellow crookneck squash
- = yellow straightneck squash
- = zucchini

❖ Peaches ❖

1 lb. = 4 medium

1 lb. = 2 cups, sliced, peeled

Peaches
- = nectarines
- = cantaloupe (in an ice, primarily)

Peanut Butter
- = sesame paste
- = other nut butters

❖ Peanuts ❖

1 lb. shelled = 2¼ cups

Pear-Apples

See Asian Pears

Pears

= Asian pears

= apples

❖ Peas ❖

1 lb. in pod = 1 cup shelled

❖ Pecans ❖

1 lb. shelled = 3 to 4 cups nutmeats

Pecans

= walnuts, in small amounts

Pepino or Melon Pears

- = pears with vanilla
- = melon

Pepper

See Black Pepper, Cayenne Pepper, Hot Red Pepper, Red Pepper

Lemon Pepper

3 tablespoons freshly ground pepper

3 tablespoons lemon zest

1 tablespoon chopped chives

Spicy Pepper Shake

1 tablespoon cayenne pepper

2 tablespoons garlic powder

2 tablespoons paprika

2 tablespoons parsley

2 tablespoons ground black pepper

½ tablespoon salt (optional)

Peppercorns

See Black Peppercorns, Green Peppercorns, White Peppercorns

Pepperoni

= sausage, cooked

= salami

Peppers

See Chile or Chili Peppers, Green Peppers, Red Peppers, Yellow Peppers

Persimmon

= puréed, cooked squash or pumpkin, sweetened

= mashed banana plus drained, canned, crushed pineapple

= mango (in recipes)

Pesto

2 cups fresh basil leaves, washed and thoroughly dried

2 cloves garlic

½ cup olive oil

1 cup freshly grated Parmesan or Romano cheese

½ cup toasted pine nuts or shelled walnuts (optional)

Process in a blender or food processor until smooth. Serve at room temperature. Yields 2 cups.

Pickling Spice

4 3-inch cinnamon sticks

1 1-inch piece dried ginger root

2 tablespoons mustard seed

2 teaspoons whole allspice

2 teaspoons black peppercorns

2 teaspoons whole cloves

2 teaspoons dill seed

2 teaspoons coriander seed

2 teaspoons whole mace, crumbled

8 bay leaves, crumbled

1 whole 1½-inch dried red pepper, chopped

Combine ingredients. Yields ⅔ cup.

Pied de Mouton or Hedgehog Mushrooms

= chanterelles

Pie Spice, Pumpkin or Apple

½ teaspoon cinnamon

¼ teaspoon nutmeg

⅛ teaspoon allspice

⅛ teaspoon cardamom

¼ teaspoon ground cloves

Combine spices. Yields enough for one 9-inch pie.

Pimento

= sweet red peppers, roasted and peeled

Pineapple Guava

= pineapple plus strawberry with a touch of banana

= pineapple, grape, lemon, and mint

Pine Nuts or Pignoli

= chopped walnuts for pesto and other Mediterranean-type recipes

= blanched, peeled, slivered almonds

Pink Beans

= pinto beans

= red beans

= kidney beans (these are larger)

Pinto Beans

- = pink beans
- = red beans
- = kidney beans (these are larger)

Pita Bread

- = flour tortillas

Plantains or Platanos

- = sweet potatoes or parsnips

Note: Use cooked only

Polenta

- = cornmeal
- = grits

Pomegranate Juice

- = grenadine plus lemon juice

Pomelo or Pummelo

- = grapefruit

Ponzu Sauce

2 parts soy sauce

1 part lemon juice

Combine.

Porcini Mushrooms

= shiitake mushrooms

= cèpe or boletus mushrooms

Pork, ground

= sausage meat (omit salt and other spices from recipe)

Pork Fat, fresh

= salt pork, boiled briefly (omit salt from recipe)

= unsmoked bacon, boiled briefly (omit salt from recipe)

Port

= Madeira

= sherry

= Marsala

❖ Potatoes ❖

1 lb. = 3 medium

1 lb. = 3 cups sliced

1 lb. = 2¼ cups cooked

1 lb. = 1¾ cups mashed

Poultry Seasoning

2 tablespoons dried marjoram

2 tablespoons dried savory

2 teaspoons dried parsley

1 tablespoon dried sage

1½ teaspoons dried thyme

Combine. Yields ⅓ cup.

Prawns

= shrimp

Prosciutto

= smoked ham or country ham

Prunes

= dates

= raisins

= dried apricots

Note: If less than ¼ cup, can be omitted from recipe.

Pumpkin

= acorn squash

= butternut squash

= turban squash (good for pies)

❖ Prunes ❖

1 lb. = 2¼ cups pitted

Q

Quail

= Cornish game hen

= squab

Quatre Épices

¼ teaspoon pepper

¼ teaspoon nutmeg

¼ teaspoon ginger

¼ teaspoon cloves

or

Use allspice.

Quince

    = golden delicious apples

    = Bartlett pears

Quinoa

    = couscous

    = millet

    See Rice

R

Rabbit

    = chicken pieces

Radicchio

    See Lettuce

Radish

    = daikon radish

    = grated horseradish

    = jicama for texture only

❖ Raisins ❖

1 lb. = 2¾ cups

Raisins, 1 cup

= 1 cup currants

= 1 cup soft prunes or dates, finely chopped

Note: If less than ½ cup, can be omitted from recipe.

Rapini

See Greens

Raspberries

= blackberries

= boysenberries

Red Beans

= pinto beans

= pink beans

= kidney beans (these are larger)

Red Cabbage

= green cabbage

Red Onions

= Bermuda onions

= Maui onions

= Vidalia onions

See Onions (Sweet)

Red Pepper, ground

- = cayenne pepper
- = chili powder
- = hot pepper sauce
- = bottled hot sauce
- = hot red pepper flakes

Red Pepper Flakes, Hot

- = chopped, dried red pepper pods
- = red pepper (use less)

Red Pepper Oil

See Chile (or Chili) Oil

Red Pepper Sauce, Hot

See Hot Pepper Sauce

Red Peppers, Sweet

- = green peppers
- = yellow peppers

Note: This is for bell peppers, not chile or chili peppers.

❖ Rice ❖

1 cup uncooked = 3 cups cooked

1 lb. = 2 to 2½ cups uncooked

Rice

The following prepared grains may be served instead of rice—or rice can be substituted for them in recipes:

barley

bulgur

couscous

millet

quinoa

Rice, "risotto" or arborio

= short-grain white rice

= short-grain brown rice

Seasoned Rice Vinegar

3 tablespoons white wine vinegar

1 tablespoon sugar

½ teaspoon salt

Combine. Yields ¼ cup.

Rice Wine

See Sake

Rocket

See Arugula

Romaine

See Lettuce

Rosemary

= marjoram

= oregano

Rutabaga or Swede

= turnip

Rum

= brandy

= cognac

S

Safflower or Azafran

= saffron (use only a tiny bit)

Saffron, ⅛ teaspoon

= 1 teaspoon dried yellow marigold petals

= 1 teaspoon azafran or safflower

= ½ to 1 teaspoon achiote seeds

= ½ to 1 teaspoon turmeric (for color)

Sage

= rosemary

= oregano

Sake

= very dry sherry or vermouth

= jui or Chinese rice wine

Salami

= pepperoni

Salsa

4 tomatoes, fresh or canned, chopped

½ cup green or red onions, chopped

¼ cup cilantro, chopped

2 cloves garlic, minced

1 teaspoon salt

1 small jalapeño pepper, seeded and chopped

2 tablespoons lime juice or red wine vinegar

1 teaspoon olive oil

Combine all ingredients. Makes 1½ to 2 cups.

Salsify or Oyster Plant

= parsnip (needs a longer cooking time)

Salt, as a flavor enhancer

= black pepper

= garlic

= onion powder

= mustard powder

= paprika

= red pepper

= lemon juice

= vinegar

= wine (not cooking wines)

Salt

= soy sauce

Salt Substitute I

1 tablespoon garlic powder

1 tablespoon powdered or crushed dried basil

1 tablespoon powdered or crushed dried oregano

½ tablespoon finely minced, dried lemon zest

 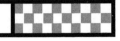

Salt Substitute II

1 tablespoon ground pepper

1 tablespoon celery seed

1 tablespoon ground coriander

2 tablespoons paprika

3 tablespoons crushed, dried summer savory

Salt, Kosher

= table salt (use less)

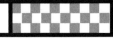

Salt, Seasoned

1 cup salt

2½ teaspoons paprika

2 teaspoons dry mustard

1½ teaspoons oregano

1 teaspoon garlic powder

1 teaspoon onion powder

or

½ cup salt

2 teaspoons ground pepper, black or white

2 teaspoons celery seeds

2 teaspoons cumin

2 teaspoons paprika

a pinch of sugar (optional)

For spicy seasoned salt, add 1 or 2 teaspoons cayenne pepper

Sapote

= mango with vanilla or vanilla custard

= a mixture of peaches, lemon, and vanilla custard

Sardines, processed

- = small herring
- = small mackerel

Sassafras

- = gumbo filé

Satsuma

- = clementine
- = orange

Sausage

- = pepperoni
- = ground pork with sage, marjoram, garlic, and onions to taste

Savory, Summer

- = thyme plus mint
- = sage

Savory, Winter

- = pepper

Scallions

- = green onions
- = shallots
- = leeks
- = onions (use less)

Scallops

= shark

Seltzer

See Club Soda

Semolina

= farina or similar breakfast cereal

= cream of wheat

Sesame Seed

= finely chopped almonds

Shallots

= green onions

= leeks

= onions (use less)

= scallions (use more)

Sherry

= Madeira

= port

= Marsala

Shiitake Mushrooms

= porcini mushrooms (cèpe or boletus)

= meat, especially steak or veal

Shortening

See Butter, Margarine

Shortening, in baking, 1 cup

= 1 cup butter

= 1 cup margarine

Shrimp

= prawns

Snow Peas

= sugar snap peas

Sorrel

= spinach (add lemon)

See Greens, Lettuce

Sour Cream, 1 cup

= 1 tablespoon white vinegar plus enough milk to make 1 cup; let stand 5 minutes before using

= 1 tablespoon lemon juice plus enough evaporated milk to make 1 cup

= 1 cup plain yogurt, especially in dips and cold soups

= cottage cheese, mixed with yogurt, if desired, and 2 tablespoons milk and 1 tablespoon lemon juice; blend well

= 6 ounces cream cheese plus 3 tablespoons milk

= ⅓ cup melted butter plus ¾ cup sour milk, for baking

Sour Milk, 1 cup

= 1½ tablespoons lemon juice or vinegar plus enough milk to make 1 cup

Note: With pasteurized milk, this is the only way to make sour milk. Pasteurized milk will spoil, but it will not go sour like raw milk.

Soursop or Sweetsop or Guanabana

= cherimoya

= custard apples

= melons and peaches

= guavas and peaches

Soy Beans or Soya (fresh)

= lima beans

= broad beans

= fava beans

Soy Sauce

3 tablespoons Worcestershire sauce

1 tablespoon water

Combine. Yields ¼ cup.

Note: Light and dark soy sauce can be substituted for each other.

Indonesian-style Soy Sauce

½ cup soy sauce

¼ cup dark brown sugar

3 tablespoons dark corn syrup

1 tablespoon molasses

Combine. Makes ¾ cup.

❖ Spaghetti ❖

1 lb. = 6½ cups cooked

Spaghetti

See Pasta

❖ Spinach ❖

1 lb. fresh = 2 cups cooked

Spinach

See Greens

Split Peas

> = mung beans, in salads

> = lentils, in soups or stews

Sprouts

> *The following sprouts are interchangeable:*
>
> alfalfa
>
> bean
>
> buckwheat
>
> sunflower
>
> **Note:** Radish sprouts are spicy.

Squab

> = Cornish game hen

> = chicken halves

> = grouse

> = pigeon

> = quail

Squash, Summer

(Small, with tender edible skin, soft seeds, picked when young)

> chayote or mirliton or christophine
>
> marrow
>
> pattypan or white squash
>
> yellow squash (straight or crooked neck)
>
> zucchini or courgettes

 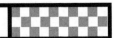

Squash, Winter

(Tough shell, firm flesh, picked when mature)

- acorn
- Australian blue
- banana
- buttercup
- butternut
- calabazo or West Indian pumpkin or Cuban squash
- delicata or sweet potato squash
- golden nugget
- hubbard
- kabocha
- pumpkin
- spaghetti squash
- sweet dumpling squash
- table queen
- turban

Star Anise or Anise Seed

= fennel seed

Starfruit or Carambola

= watermelon with lemon juice

Stock, Chicken, Beef, Veal, Fish

= bouillon

= consommé

Note: Stock in a sauce may be replaced by wine for up to
⅓ of stock required.

❖ Sugar ❖

Granulated white, 1 lb. = 2 cups

Powdered or confectioners, 1 lb. = 3½ to 4 cups

Firmly packed brown, 1 lb. = 2¼ cups

Sugar, Brown, ½ cup

= ½ cup white sugar plus 2 tablespoons molasses

Note: To replace a combination of brown sugar and milk,
use honey or molasses with powdered milk.

Sugar, Granulated White, 1 cup

= 1 cup superfine sugar

= 1 cup turbinado sugar

= 1 cup firmly packed brown sugar

= 2 cups powdered sugar, sifted

= ¾ cup honey or 1¼ cups molasses and reduce other
liquid in recipe by ¼ cup; or add ¼ cup flour if no
other liquid is called for

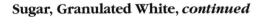

Sugar, Granulated White, *continued*

> = 1 cup corn syrup, but never replace more than half the amount of sugar this way; always reduce the other liquid in the recipe by ¼ cup for each 2 cups sugar substituted this way

Note:

- Sugar generally may be reduced by a quarter of the amount.
- Sugar can be reduced by ½ cup if liquid is reduced by ¼ cup.
- A few tablespoons of granulated sugar may be replaced by maple sugar.
- Sugar substitutions tend to make baked goods heavier.
- Write to manufacturers of artificial sweeteners for recipes using those products.

Sugar, Superfine

> = granulated sugar

Note: Granulated sugar may take longer to dissolve.

Vanilla Sugar

2 cups sugar

2 vanilla beans

Store in an airtight container. Replenish sugar as used until vanilla has been depleted.

Sugar Snap Peas

= snow peas

Sumac

= zaatar

= lemongrass

= lemon

= verbena

Summer Savory

Thyme (*Optional:* add sage)

Summer Squash or Pattypan Squash

= yellow crook neck squash

= yellow straight neck squash

= zucchini

Sunchokes

See Jerusalem Artichokes

Sunflower Sprouts

= watercress

See Sprouts

Swede

See Rutabaga

Sweet Potatoes

= yams

Swiss Chard

See Greens

T

Tahini

- = ground sesame seed
- = unsalted sunflower seeds or blanched almonds, ground with a little vegetable oil

Tamarind and Tamarind Paste

- = dried apricots, dates, and lemon juice
- = chopped prunes and lemon juice

Tamarind, pods

- = lemon juice

Taro or Edo

- = dasheen
- = potato
- = parsnip

Tarragon

- = anise (use less)
- = Mexican mint marigold
- = chervil (use more)
- = parsley (use more)

Tartar Sauce

2 tablespoons sweet pickle relish or sweet pickles, chopped

4 tablespoons mayonnaise

1 tablespoon onion, chopped (optional)

1 tablespoon hard-boiled egg, chopped (optional)

a few drops lemon juice (optional)

½ teaspoon mustard

Combine. Makes ½ cup.

❖ Tea ❖

1 lb. leaves = 100 servings

Teriyaki Sauce

5 tablespoons soy sauce

3 tablespoons seasoned rice vinegar

1 teaspoon ginger, powdered or fresh, minced

Combine. Yields ½ cup.

Thousand Island Dressing

1 cup mayonnaise

½ cup chili sauce

¼ cup ketchup

1 tablespoon pickle relish

Combine ingredients. Makes 1¾ cups.

Thyme

- = marjoram
- = oregano
- = savory
- = bay leaf

Tomatillos

- = fresh green tomatoes plus lemon juice
- = pickled green tomatoes

❖ Tomatoes ❖

1 lb. = 2 to 3 medium

1 lb. = 1 8-oz. can

1 lb. = 1 cup chopped

Tomatoes, canned, 1 cup

= 1⅓ cups chopped fresh tomatoes, simmered

Tomatoes, cooked, seasoned, 1 lb.

= 8 ounces tomato sauce, for cooking

Tomato Juice, 1 cup

= 2 or 3 fresh, ripe tomatoes, peeled, seeded, and blended in blender or food processor (add salt and lemon juice to taste)

= ½ cup tomato sauce plus ½ cup water

Tomato Paste, 1 tablespoon

= 1 tablespoon ketchup

= ¼ cup tomato sauce (and reduce some other liquid from recipe)

Tomato Purée, 1 cup

= 1 cup tomato sauce

= ½ cup tomato paste plus ½ cup water

Tomato Sauce, 2 cups

= ¾ cup tomato paste plus 1 cup water

= 2 cups tomato purée

Tortillas

= pita bread, split

Triticale, flaked

= rolled oats

Triticale Berries

= wheat berries

Truffles, fresh

= canned truffles or canned truffle peels; add canning liquid

Note: The above substitution is nowhere near the fresh. Truffles are in season in the fall.

Turmeric

= mustard powder

(*Optional:* add saffron)

Tuna, canned

= albacore

= cooked, boned chicken

Turnips, for cooking

= rutabaga

= kohlrabi

Turnips, raw

= jicama

= radish

Turnip Greens

See Greens

Twentieth Century Pears

See Asian Pears

U

Ugli or Ugli Fruit

= grapefruit plus sugar

V

Vanilla Extract, in baking

= almond extract

= peppermint or other extracts (use less). This will alter the flavor of the product.

Veal, scallops

= boned, skinned chicken breasts

= turkey breast slices

Verbena

= lemon peel

= lemongrass

= sumac

Vermicelli

See Pasta

Vidalia Onions

See Onions (Sweet)

Vienna Sausages

= frankfurters

Vinegar

= lemon juice, in cooking and salads

= grapefruit juice, in salads

= wine, in marinades

Vinegar, Apple Cider

= champagne vinegar

= malt vinegar

= rice vinegar

Vinegar, Balsamic

= sherry vinegar

Vinegar, Champagne

= apple cider vinegar

Vinegar, Malt

= apple cider vinegar

Vinegar, Red Wine

= white wine vinegar

Vinegar, Rice

= apple cider vinegar

Vinegar, Sherry

= balsamic vinegar

Vinegar, White Wine

= red wine vinegar

Walla Walla Onions

See Onions (Sweet)

Wasabi, powdered

= hot dry mustard

Wasabi, prepared, 1 tablespoon

= 1 tablespoon hot dry mustard plus 1½ teaspoons
vinegar plus 1 teaspoon oil plus ¼ teaspoon salt

Water Chestnuts

= jicama, raw

Watercress

= sunflower sprouts

See Lettuce

Wax Beans

= green beans

Whiskey

= bourbon

White Beans

= pea beans

= navy beans

White Peppercorns

= black peppercorns

Note: Peppercorns vary in strength.

Wine, for marinades, ½ cup

= ¼ cup vinegar plus 1 tablespoon sugar plus ¼ cup water

Winter Melon

= zucchini

= fuzzy melon

= chayote

Wood Ear Mushroom

= cloud ear

= black fungus or silver ear

Worcestershire Sauce

1 teaspoon soy sauce

2 drops hot pepper sauce

1 dash lemon juice

1 pinch sugar or 1 dash molasses

Combine. Makes 1½ teaspoons.

Y

Yams

= sweet potatoes

❖ Yeast, Compressed, 1 cake ❖

= 2 envelopes dry yeast

= 2 tablespoons powdered yeast

❖ Yeast, Dry, 1 envelope ❖

= 1 tablespoon powdered yeast

= ½ cake compressed yeast, crumbled

Yellow Finn Potatoes

= 2 parts white potatoes plus 1 part yams or sweet potatoes

Yellow or Gold Peppers

= red peppers

= green peppers

Yellow Squash, Crookneck or Straightneck

= pattypan squash

= zucchini

Yogurt, Plain

= sour cream

= crème fraiche

= buttermilk

= heavy cream

= mayonnaise (in small amounts, especially in salads or dips)

Z

Zaatar (Middle Eastern Spice Blend)

= sumac plus savory plus roasted sesame seed

Zucchini

= pattypan squash

= yellow crookneck squash

= yellow straightneck squash

Too Much

Sometimes, instead of not having a particular ingredient at all, you have the opposite problem: You end up with too much of something. The following is designed to remedy common kitchen disasters of this type.

Alcohol

If too much in punch or other mixed alcoholic drinks, float thin slices of cucumber to absorb the taste of alcohol.

Fat, in stew, soup, or gravy

Drop in ice cubes; the grease will stick to them. Remove quickly.

or

Wrap ice cubes in paper towels and draw over the surface. The fat will begin to solidify and stick to the paper towel. Repeat until enough fat is removed.

or

Place paper towel lightly on surface and allow to absorb fat, then remove. Repeat as necessary.

or

Use a flat lettuce leaf the same way.

or

Refrigerate dish. When cool, skim solidified fat from the top surface. Continue with recipe.

Garlic

Simmer a sprig or small bunch of parsley in stew or soup for ten minutes.

To remove onion and garlic flavors from hands, pots and pans, chopping boards, etc., rub with salt, lemon juice, or vinegar.

Ketchup, in a sauce

Add lemon juice to mask some of the ketchupy taste. You may add a bit of sugar to cut the lemon's acidity.

Salt

Add a peeled, thinly sliced potato to the salty dish and boil until the potato is transparent. Remove the potato slices.

or

If fish is too salty, add vinegar to the cooking liquid.

or

For a tomato dish, add more peeled tomatoes to absorb the salt. Leave in dish if appropriate.

or

For items like soup, stew, or tomato sauce, add pinches of brown sugar to taste.

Tomato

Add lemon juice to mask some of the tomato taste. Add a bit of sugar to cut the lemon's acidity.

Too Spicy

In the pot, add salt.

On the tongue, lips, or mouth, a little sugar, buttermilk, milk, bread, or crackers will help neutralize the spiciness.

Measurement Equivalents

Here is a list of commonly used measuring equivalents for the kitchen.

Food Measuring Equivalents

Dry Measures

1 pinch = ⅛ teaspoon, approximately

½ tablespoon = 1½ teaspoons

3 teaspoons = 1 tablespoon

¼ cup = 4 tablespoons

⅓ cup = 5 tablespoons + 1 teaspoon

⅜ cup = 6 tablespoons

½ cup = 8 tablespoons

⅔ cup = 10 tablespoons + 2 teaspoons

¾ cup = 12 tablespoons

1 cup = 16 tablespoons

4 cups = 1 quart

8 quarts = 1 peck*

4 pecks = 1 bushel*

* for large fruits and vegetables, not berries

Liquid Measures

1 dash = a few drops, approximately

1 tablespoon = 3 teaspoons

1 tablespoon = ½ fluid ounce

1 fluid ounce = 2 tablespoons

1 jigger = 3 tablespoons or 1½ fluid ounces

¼ cup = 4 tablespoons or 2 fluid ounces

½ cup = 8 tablespoons or 4 fluid ounces

1 cup = 16 tablespoons or 8 fluid ounces

1 pint = 2 cups or 16 fluid ounces

1 quart = 2 pints or 32 fluid ounces

1 gallon = 4 quarts or 64 fluid ounces

Fluid Ounces	=	Milliliters
1		30
2		60
4		120
6		180
8 (1 cup)		235
16 (1 pint)		475
32 (1 quart)		945

Note: 1 quart = .946 liter

1 liter = 1.057 quarts

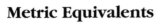
Metric Equivalents

Ounces	=	Grams
1		28
2		57
3		85
4		113
5		142
6		170
7		198
8		227
9		255
10		284
11		312
12		340
13		368
14		397
15		425
16		454

Grams	=	Ounces
1		.035
50		1.75
100		3.5
250		8.75
500		17.5
750		26.25
1000		35
(1 kilogram)		(2.21 lbs.)

Metric Equivalents

Pounds	=	Kilograms
1		.45
2		.91
3		1.4
4		1.8
5		2.3
6		2.7
7		3.2
8		3.5
9		4.1
10		4.5

Kilograms	=	Pounds
1		2.2
2		4.4
3		6.6
4		8.8
5		11

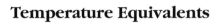
Temperature Equivalents

	Degrees Fahrenheit	=	Degrees Celsius (Centigrade)
Room Temperature	70		21
Lukewarm	90		32
Water's Boiling Point	212		100
Low or Cool Oven	250		120
Slow Oven	300		150
Moderately Slow Oven	325		165
Moderate Oven	350		180
Moderately Hot Oven	375		190
Hot Oven	400		205
Very Hot Oven	450–500		230–360
Broil	550		290

Baking Pan Sizes

Note: Adjust baking times when changing pan sizes.

Cake Pans, Rectangular

8" x 8" x 2"

    = 6 cups

    = 20 cm x 20 cm x 5 cm

9" x 9" x 1½ "

    = 6 cups

    = 23 cm x 23 cm x 4 cm

9" x 9" x 2"

    = 7 cups

    = 23 cm x 23 cm x 5 cm

13" x 9" x 2"

    = 10 cups

    = 33 cm x 23 cm x 5 cm

Cake Pans, Round

8" x 1½"

    = 4 cups

    = 20 cm x 4 cm

9" x 1½"

    = 6 cups

    = 23 cm x 4 cm

 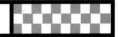

Loaf Pans

8½" x 4½" x 2½"

    = 6 cups

    = 22 cm x 11 cm x 6 cm

9" x 5" x 3"

    = 8 cups

    = 23 cm x 13 cm x 8 cm

Pie Pans

8" x 1¼"

    = 3 cups, level

    = 4½ cups, mounded

    = 20 cm x 3 cm

9" x 1½"

    = 4 cups, level

    = 5 to 6 cups, mounded

    = 23 cm x 4 cm

Springform Pans

8" x 3"

    = 10 cups

    = 20 cm x 8 cm

9" x 3"

    = 11 cups

    = 23 cm x 9 cm

Spring Form Pans, *continued*

10" x 3¾"

    = 12 cups

    = 25 cm x 10 cm

Tube Pans or Ring Molds

8½" x 2¼"

    = 41½ cups

    = 22 cm x 6 cm

7½" x 3"

    = 6 cups

    = 19 cm x 8 cm

9¼" x 2¾"

    = 8 cups

    = 23 cm x 7 cm

Household Formulas

You probably know what it feels like to be standing in the supermarket, not wanting to spend a small fortune on the lastest specialty cleanser just to see if maybe it works.

We have discovered that many common household items, such as vinegar and baking soda, make great substitutes for commercial cleaning products. You'll find them not only effective, but inexpensive.

Look down this list, and chances are you'll find a tried-and-true recipe for just what you need. Many of these substitutions for cleansers are non-toxic alternatives—and thus kinder to both people and the environment.

Air Freshener

Bake orange peels at 350 degrees for 10 minutes.

or

Place a sliced orange, grapefruit or lemon in a pan of water and boil gently for an hour.

or

Place bowls of baking soda or activated charcoal around the house.

or

Pour vinegar into an uncovered dish.

Air Freshener Spray

In a spray bottle dissolve 1 teaspoon baking soda and 1 teaspoon lemon juice in 2 cups hot water.

All-Purpose Cleanser

½ cup Borax

1 gallon warm water

or

½ cup ammonia

¼ cup vinegar

2 tablespoons baking soda

1 gallon warm water

Note: Good for floors.

or

½ cup ammonia

½ cup washing soda

1 gallon warm water

Bathroom Cleanser

Dip damp sponge in baking soda.

Black Lacquer Cleanser

Dip a cloth in a strong tea solution and rub well.

Brass Cleanser

Rub hard with lemon juice and salt. Or spread with ketchup, let stand 10 minutes, and then rub hard.

Breadbox Cleanser

2 tablespoons vinegar in 1 quart water.

Note: Deters mold, too.

Carpet Deodorizer

1 cup baking soda or 1 cup cornstarch

Sprinkle on carpet. Wait 30 minutes and vacuum.

Chrome Cleanser

Make a paste of baking soda and water.

or

Use the fresh-squeezed rind of a lemon.

or

Use vinegar.

Copper Cleanser

Spread with a paste of lemon juice, salt, and flour, or spread with ketchup. Let stand 10 minutes and rub hard.

Crystal Cleanser

Use a mixture of half rubbing alcohol, half water.
Do not rinse.

Cutting Boards

Rub with baking soda. Spray with vinegar, let sit 5 minutes and rinse with water.

Deodorant

After bathing, sprinkle some baking soda in your hands and rub under your arms.

Disinfectant

Use ½ cup Borax in 1 gallon hot water.

Drain Cleaner

½ cup salt

½ cup vinegar

Pour down drain, followed by 2 quarts boiling water.

Drain Freshener

Pour ½ cup baking soda down the drain. After 2 minutes pour in ½ cup vinegar followed by 2 quarts of boiling water.

Drain Opener

Dump 1 cup baking soda down drain, followed by 1 cup vinegar. Cover drain. When fizzing stops, pour boiling water down drain.

Dusting Cloth

Lightly moisten cloth with a mixture of equal parts olive oil and vinegar.

Electric Iron Stain Remover

Use equal parts vinegar and salt.

Fertilizer

1 tablespoon Epsom salts

1 tablespoon baking soda

1½ teaspoons household ammonia

3 gallons water

Floor Cleaner

½ cup vinegar

½ gallon warm water

or

¼ cup washing soda

½ tablespoon liquid soap

¼ cup vinegar

2 gallons hot water

Floor Shiner

½ cup cornstarch

1 gallon lukewarm water

Furniture Cleaner

1 cup cooled strong black tea

¼ cup vinegar

Furniture Polish

⅔ cup olive oil (or mineral or linseed oil)

⅓ cup lemon juice or 1 teaspoon lemon oil

or

Walnut oil

Hard Water Deposit Remover

Soak item in white vinegar or a half-and-half solution of white vinegar and water.

Mildew Remover

½ cup vinegar

½ cup Borax

Warm water

Mouthwash

Gargle with equal parts hydrogen peroxide and water.

Note: Do not swallow.

Mouth Freshener

Chew on a sprig of parsley, or cloves.

Non-Stick Pan Cleanser

Use baking soda on a non-abrasive scouring pad.

Oven Cleaner, for non-self-cleaning ovens

Pour ½ cup ammonia into a bowl. Set in cold oven overnight. Next morning, mix the ammonia with 1 quart warm water and wipe off inside of oven.

or

Mix equal parts baking soda and salt. Scrub with a damp sponge.

Pesticide for Ants

1 teaspoon liquid soap

1 quart water

Mix in a spray bottle.

and

Use Vaseline or dish soap to block up entry holes.

Pesticide for Cockroaches and Silverfish

Dust cracks and crevices with a fine layer of boric acid.

Note: Keep out of reach of children.

or

Combine equal parts sugar and baking soda and set out.

Note: Keep out of reach of children.

Pewter Polish

Mix equal parts salt and flour and make a paste using vinegar. Rub on, let dry, rinse in hot water.

or

Take dampened cabbage leaves, sprinkle them with salt and rub on the pewter.

Pot and Pan Cleanser

Soak in white vinegar for 30 minutes.

Refrigerator Cleanser

1 tablespoon Borax

1 quart water

or

1 teaspoon baking soda

1 quart water

Refrigerator Deodorizer

Place opened container of baking soda in refrigerator or freezer.

or

Place dampened, crumpled newspapers in refrigerator. Replace every 24 hours until smell is gone.

or

Place slices of white bread in the refrigerator.

Scouring Powder

Use baking soda.

or

1 cup baking soda

1 cup salt

Mix together. Store in an airtight container.

Silver Cleanser

Make paste of baking soda and water. Apply with damp sponge or cloth and continue rubbing until clean.

or

Use toothpaste and a soft-bristled toothbrush.

Silver Polish

Place silver in a pan and cover with water. Add 2 tablespoons salt, 2 tablespoons baking soda, and a few sheets of aluminum foil. Let stand for an hour or more until tarnish disappears.

or

Add a few drops of vegetable oil to a small amount of toothpaste and polish with a soft toothbrush.

or

For silver jewelry: soak in lemon juice or vinegar.

Soft Scrub

Make a paste from ½ cup baking soda and liquid soap.

Spot and Blood Remover

½ cup Borax

2 cups cold water

Spray Cleaner, Grease Cutting

1 quart hot water

2 teaspoons Borax

1 teaspoon washing soda

¼ cup vinegar

1 teaspoon liquid soap

Combine in a spray bottle.

Spray Cleaner, Super Clean

1 quart hot water

1 tablespoon Borax

⅜ cup vinegar

Combine in a spray bottle.

Stainless Steel Cleanser

Use ammonia and hot water, mixed with a mild, non-chlorinated cleanser.

or

To remove spots, rub with a cloth dampened with white vinegar.

Stain Remover, Blood

Use hydrogen peroxide.

or

Soak with ½ cup Borax dissolved in 2 cups cold water.

or

Make a paste of cornstarch or talcum powder and water. Let dry on stain and brush off.

Stain Remover, Blood, *continued*

or

Sprinkle with meat tenderizer and water. Sponge off after 30 minutes.

Stain Remover, Chocolate

Use hydrogen peroxide.

Stain Remover, Coffee

Rub fabric with cloth saturated with beaten egg yoke or denatured alcohol. Rinse with water.

or

Make a paste of Borax and hot water and rub into the stain.

or

Dampen with club soda and sprinkle with salt.

Stain Remover, Fruit and Wine

Dampen with club soda.

Stain Remover, Grass

Soak in vinegar.

Stain Remover, Grease

Sprinkle fabric with cornmeal or cornstarch or talcum powder. After 12 hours brush off.

or

Dampen with club soda.

Stain Remover, Ink

Soak in milk.

or

Soak in lemon juice.

Stain Remover, Perspiration

Make a paste of salt and water and rub on stain.

or

Make a paste of baking soda and salt and rub on stain.

or

Use vinegar.

Stain Remover, Tea

Pour very hot water on fabric from a height of at least 2 feet.

Toilet Bowl Cleanser

4 tablespoons baking soda plus 1 cup vinegar

or

1 cup Borax. Let sit overnight.

Toothpaste

Make a paste of baking soda and water.

or

Make a paste of baking soda, salt, and water.

Tub and Tile Cleanser

Rub with half a lemon dipped in Borax.

Water Spots on Dishes

Add vinegar to rinse water.

Water Stains on Furniture

Rub with toothpaste.

Window Cleanser

Mix ½ cup white or cider vinegar in ½ gallon water.

Spray on windows and wipe with crumpled newspaper.

or

Use ½ cup cornstarch in 2 quarts warm water.

or

Use 1 tablespoon ammonia in 2 cups water. Wear protective gloves while you clean.

Woodwork Cleanser

1 teaspoon white vinegar

1 quart water

Woodwork (Varnished), Furniture, or Glass Cleanser

Tea, steeped 30 to 40 minutes

About the Authors

BECKY SUE EPSTEIN is a marketing consultant and wine and food writer, formerly based in Los Angeles. Her writing has appeared in *Food & Wine* magazine, *The Los Angeles Times,* and *The Boston Globe.* She recently relocated to Boston, where she continues to serve on the Board of Directors of the American Institute of Wine and Food.

HILARY DOLE KLEIN is a travel writer, columnist, and food reviewer, currently residing in Santa Barbara, California. She has written articles for *Islands* magazine, *Food & Wine* magazine, *The Los Angeles Times,* and the *Santa Barbara Independent.* She has written or edited seven books, including *Santa Barbara Cooks, Tiny Game Hunting,* and the *1996 New Zealand Vacation Planner.*